A Moment with God

for Teachers

PRAYERS FOR
EVERY TEACHER

W9-CFJ-459

DIMENSIONS
FOR LIVING
NASHVILLE

A MOMENT WITH GOD FOR TEACHERS

Copyright © 1998 by Dimensions for Living

This book is printed on recycled, acid-free paper.

Library of Congress Cataloging-in-Publication Data

A moment with God for teachers : prayers for every teacher.
　　p.　cm.
　Prayers were written by Karen Cropsey, Lori Gribble, and Sallie Dye.
　ISBN 0-687-07710-9 (hardback : alk. paper)
　1. Teachers—Prayer-books and devotions—English.　I. Crospey, Karen.　II. Gribble, Lori.　III. Dye, Sallie.
BV4596.T43M66　　1998
242′.88—dc21　　　　　　　　　　　　　　　　97-47068

Prayers appearing on pages 7–59 were written by Karen Cropsey. Those on pages 60–63 were written by Lori Gribble. That on page 64 was written by Sallie Dye.

99 00 01 02 03 04 05 06 07 — 10 9 8 7 6 5 4 3

MANUFACTURED IN THE UNITED STATES OF AMERICA

CONTENTS

FOR ELEMENTARY SCHOOL TEACHERS

I will instruct you and teach you the way you should go. —Psalm 32:8a

Lord, it is not easy to be both teacher and surrogate parent. My classroom is filled with children who spend more time with me than they do with their families. Give us the loving hands we need to guide young minds to adulthood by starting them on the right path. The children are sometimes like Thomas—doubting everything; sometimes like Pilate—so condemning; sometimes like the rich young ruler—refusing to give up "riches" in order to enter the Kingdom. Teachers need the wisdom of Solomon and the patience of Job. Help us to be like Peter, the Rock, so that we may be the foundation in the lives of the students who depend on us so much. Amen.

FOR JUNIOR HIGH SCHOOL TEACHERS

Let all that you do be done in love.
—1 Corinthians 16:14

Lord, sometimes it seems that we have the most difficult job of all teachers. Our pupils are too old to play and too young to drive. They live in a never-land of in-betweeness that seems to go on forever. Help me to help them realize that as their bodies are growing and developing, they are adjusting to the next stage in their lives.

Let me give them respect and treat them fairly as a means of understanding this difficult period of adjustment. Let me be like Jesus as he washed the feet of the disciples, showing how much he cared for them. By humbling myself, perhaps my students will be humbled and know that I care for them for who they are. Amen.

FOR HIGH SCHOOL TEACHERS

Let us therefore no longer pass judgment on one another, but resolve instead never to put a stumbling block or hindrance in the way of another. —Romans 14:13

Lord, dealing with young adults is such a difficult joy! Give us the strength to understand the pressures of adolescence, to remember the problems of puberty and peer pressure. It is so hard not to judge—and even more difficult to give so much of ourselves to those who sometimes care so little. High school students need guidance in figuring out who they are and where they are in your world and, even more important, where they belong. Let my classroom be a door, and help me to realize that the students who enter are knocking for more than just education; they are knocking for life itself! Amen.

THE FIRST DAY OF SCHOOL

Everything old has passed away; see, everything has become new!

—*2 Corinthians 5:17*

Lord, help me to remember how it was when I sat on the other side of the desk. Remind me that I was frightened and fragile—anxious to begin the next grade and learn new things; afraid that the new grade would be too hard and the work would be overwhelming. Help me to remember that I am teaching people, not pages and workbooks. Enable me to remember this throughout the new year and to make coming to school each day a joy for my students. Amen.

BEFORE
THE CHRISTMAS HOLIDAYS

"To you is born this day in the city of David a Savior, who is the Messiah, the Lord."
—Luke 2:11

Lord, as we break for this holiday season, let the children know the joy of your birth. Help them to return after the break as you came to us—in innocence and purity. Enable me to give them the gift of learning, just as you gave the gift of yourself. You held nothing back; may I follow your example. Amen.

THE LAST DAY OF SCHOOL

Be renewed in the spirit of your minds, and ...
clothe yourselves with the new self, created
according to the likeness of God.
—Ephesians 4:23-24

Today I rejoice! Summer break has arrived. I thank you, Lord, for the good year my students and I have had together. The days have melted into each other since last autumn and have now disappeared into summer! Where have they gone?

It will be sad to see these children go, but it is time. I hope and pray that I have given them the wings they need to fly. Let each and every one have a safe summer, a time to enjoy the sunshine and the clouds. May they return to school next fall renewed and ready for even greater challenges than I was privileged to offer. Amen.

A MONDAY MORNING PRAYER

This one thing I do: forgetting what lies behind and straining forward to what lies ahead, I press on. —*Philippians 3:13-14*

Father, it's Monday again. I have spent the weekend working on lesson plans and grading papers. It seems that there has been no time for me to relax and forget about school. Remind me as I start this new week that I have a classroom of students waiting to see what I have planned for them and ready—I hope—to learn new things. Help me to see Monday morning as a challenge rather than a chore. Fill me with the expectation of my students as they anticipate what the week might bring. Help me to put on a smile that invites my students to share my enthusiasm. And remind me of Jesus' words, "Let the little children come to me . . . for it is to such as these that the kingdom of God belongs" (Luke 18:16). Amen.

LET THIS BE A GREAT DAY

This is the day that the LORD has made; / let us rejoice and be glad in it. —Psalm 118:24

Lord, let this be a great day. May all my students have their homework—or make me laugh at their creative excuses! May all have the things they need for the day, including lunch money, and may the sun shine long enough for the students to go outside for recess. I pray that interruptions will be minimal and that we will be able to get though the day without complaining about the work we must do.

Let the day be fun and full of adventure. May I share a story about myself that will prove to my students that I too was young once and that I understand what it's like to be a student. Let the reason that I wanted to be a teacher be obvious today to everyone around me. Amen.

BEFORE CLASS

"Let the little children come to me, and do not stop them; for it is to such as these that the kingdom of heaven belongs."
— *Matthew 19:14*

Jesus, give me your ability to teach. Help me draw the children to me as you drew them to yourself so many years ago. Stay beside me, filling me with the words that will make them understand the lessons I have planned for today. Let them know, through my actions, that I am part of you, even though I cannot openly say so. Amen.

BEFORE RECESS

I pray that all may go well with you and that you may be in good health, just as it is well with your soul.

—*3 John 2*

Lord, thank you for a time of day that lets the boys and girls run off the wiggles! It is so hard for them to sit still for so long. Let them have a good time of exercise, fresh air, and fun. Keep them safe as they play hard on the monkey bars and swings, baseball field, and basketball court. Let this time for refreshment and freedom from their studies strengthen their bodies.

Thank you, Lord, for these few minutes of relief from intense instruction! Amen.

BUS DUTY

Discipline always seems painful rather than pleasant at the time, but later it yields the peaceful fruit of righteousness to those who have been trained by it.   —Hebrews 12:11

Father, of all my "no-teaching" responsibilities, this is the one that is the hardest. Give me the discipline I need to get through the extra hours I am on my feet on the days when I have bus duty. Put joy on my face instead of resentment for not being able to take this time to prepare for class. After school, help me to wish the children well instead of pushing them along so I can hurry into my room and wrap up the day. Give me the patience to deal with parents who are never on time for afternoon pick-up; bus drivers who leave too soon, causing children to miss their ride home; and day-care van drivers who insist their riders leave first. Amen.

BEFORE A CLASS PARTY

Make a joyful noise to the LORD, all the earth.
—*Psalm 100:1*

Dear God, it's party day again. The children are so wound up and excited that they can hardly pay attention to their work. I hope the parent-helpers have planned plenty of games to keep the students involved. I hope they have enough treats and plenty of patience to deal with the fidgety little bodies awaiting them. Please prevent too many spills, and keep those who do not win prizes from having hurt feelings. Thank you, Lord, for the parent-helpers who are willing to give up their time to provide us with this celebration. Amen.

BEFORE A FIELD TRIP

Let the wise also hear and gain in learning.
—*Proverbs 1:5*a

Lord, as we leave school today, the excitement of a day of learning away from our desks is contagious. Give us the ability to listen. Help us to understand the rules of safety. Teach us that not everything we learn comes from books and workbooks, but that learning is a living, breathing experience that happens all around us every day. It is life; without it, there is no future. Amen.

BEFORE A SCHOOL PLAY/ PAGEANT/ PERFORMANCE

The one who began a good work among you will bring it to completion.

—Philippians 1:6

Today is the big day, Lord. They have rehearsed their lines. Their costumes have been prepared. Let the students do their best for their parents and friends and others who have come to see this program. Help the audience to remember that these students desire only to do well and to please them, even though they are nervous and scared—afraid they will make mistakes. Most of all, let the audience remember that they are students, not professionals. Give these performers smiling faces and happy hearts as they do their best for those they love. Amen.

BEFORE
TRACK AND FIELD DAY

"In everything do to others as you would have them do to you; for this is the law and the prophets."

—*Matthew 7:12*

Today is a day of outdoor field games and events. Lord, please be with the children and keep them safe as they compete. Let them remember and practice the rules of good sportsmanship, and remind them often of the golden rule as they strive to win. Amen.

BEFORE GRADING PAPERS

The teaching of the wise is a fountain of life.
—*Proverbs 13:14*a

A gentle tongue is a tree of life, / but perverseness in it breaks the spirit.
—*Proverbs 15:4*

Lord, why did I ask the children to do so much work today? Now, I'll be grading papers all evening. Help me to be fair, evaluate carefully each assignment, and remember that trying one's best is as important as "making the grade." May my corrections be made in love; help me to write positive comments and not focus just on the mistakes. Help me to remember that a child can be motivated or discouraged by the words I write with my grading pen. Give me stamina and perseverance, Lord, and may I look on this stack of papers not as a chore but as a reward for the work that has been learned today. Amen.

AT REPORT CARD TIME

*A fool takes no pleasure in understanding, /
but only in expressing personal opinion.*
                                    —*Proverbs 18:2*

Jesus, help me to keep you in mind as I
work on report cards. Remind me that
you were kind, compassionate, loving,
and always understanding when you dealt
with those around you. May I be the
same as I average grades and record them.
Help me see the good in each child as I
evaluate. Enable me to be fair and
objective, just as you were with
Zacchaeus. Help me to have true
understanding, seeing beyond my own
biases and opinions. And may the parents
be accepting of their children's abilities,
instead of expecting so much that their
children feel defeated. Amen.

BEFORE
ACHIEVEMENT TESTS

We do not dare to classify or compare ourselves with some of those who commend themselves. But when they measure themselves by one another, and compare themselves with one another, they do not show good sense.... "Let the one who boasts, boast in the Lord." For it is not those who commend themselves that are approved, but those whom the Lord commends.
—*2 Corinthians 10:12, 17-18*

Lord, we put so much emphasis on achievement tests. The children are showing signs of stress under the strain of trying to do well. Why is one week of testing supposed to determine what we have done in nearly a year of work? Help us all to keep these tests in perspective and to remember that they are one tool for measuring progress. Surround my soul with the peace of mind that I have done the very best I can for the students in my class. Amen.

FOR A CHILD RECEIVING
AN AWARD ON AWARDS DAY

Bless the LORD, O my soul, / and all that is within me, / bless his holy name. / Bless the LORD, O my soul, / and do not forget all his benefits.

—Psalm 103:1-2

Lord, be gracious with this child who has worked so hard. Let this child be proud of this accomplishment and remember the work that it took to get there. Let this child also remember to be thankful and to give you praise. Finally, let this child not forget that it will take more hard work to continue to achieve. Teach humility and modesty along with pride. Amen.

FOR A CHILD
NOT RECEIVING AN AWARD
ON AWARDS DAY

For it was you who formed my inward parts; / you knit me together in my mother's womb. / I praise you, for I am fearfully and wonderfully made.

—*Psalm 139:13-14*a

Lord, so many will shine today, but not all. So many will have parents to praise them today, but not all. So many will be alone, hurt, and bruised because no one seems to care—or because they didn't quite "measure up." Be with each of them, Lord, and let them know that they too are important and special and worthy of recognition. Amen.

WHEN STUDENTS
ARE DISTRACTED

Whatever is true, whatever is honorable, whatever is just, whatever is pure, whatever is pleasing, whatever is commendable, if there is any excellence and if there is anything worthy of praise, think about these things.
—*Philippians 4:8*

Lord, it is so hard to compete with TV and video games, CD players, empty stomachs, uncaring parents, and fights with siblings and friends. I know some of my students don't want to be here today. It's obvious their minds are somewhere else. When they're distracted, sometimes it's hard to keep *my* mind from wandering too. Somehow, let me be so excited about the lessons today that they will forget about the distractions and focus their minds on learning. Amen.

WHEN STUDENTS DON'T DO THEIR HOMEWORK

In all toil there is profit, / but mere talk leads only to poverty. —*Proverbs 14:23*

Lord, once again there are students who have not completed their homework. Let me be patient with them as they give excuses that have come to be so common: My mother took it out of my backpack to check it and forgot to put it back in; my little sister was playing school and wrote all over it; I had baseball practice last night; it was my night to visit my dad, and I left it at his house; I turned it in, and you lost it. Help me to remember, Lord, that sometimes there is no one at home to encourage them and help them. May I do all I can to teach them the value of discipline and hard work. Amen.

DEALING
WITH A TROUBLEMAKER

Bear with one another and, if anyone has a complaint against another, forgive each other; just as the Lord has forgiven you, so you also must forgive.

—Colossians 3:13

Lord, you know I did not want this child in my room this year; neither did anyone else. He has so many problems keeping his mouth "under control" and his hands to himself. Help me to try to understand why he acts this way, to look beyond his behavior, and to love him. Please give me what it takes to hold myself in check when the going gets tough, to forgive, and to move on. Jesus was able to do that. By following his example—with your help—I know *I* can too. Amen.

FOR A STUDENT
WHO CHEATS (COPIES)

By the open statement of the truth we commend ourselves to the conscience of everyone in the sight of God. —*2 Corinthians 4:2c*

I saw this student copy from another's paper, Lord. For what reason? Lack of study time? Lack of self-confidence? Whatever the reason, it is dishonest and cannot be allowed. Show me how to deal with this, for it is important that this student learn that actions have consequences.

Help me tell this student's parents about the incident in a nonjudgmental way and provide guidance or assistance in teaching or reinforcing important values. Keep me from overstepping my bounds and entering into the realm of parental responsibility. May my concern for the student shine through, above all else. Amen.

FOR A STUDENT WHO STEALS

Thieves must give up stealing; rather let them labor and work honestly with their own hands, so as to have something to share with the needy.
—Ephesians 4:28

Why, Lord, must he take what he knows isn't his? Is it jealously that makes him do it? Is such a small item really a "need"? Help me discipline with special care in this instance; for when stealing begins at this age, I fear a pattern may be forming. Regardless of whether this is a first-time incident or an established habit, help me to stop it carefully, for what I say and do may affect a life forever. Amen.

LOVING "THE UNLOVABLE"

"Do not judge, and you will not be judged; do not condemn, and you will not be condemned.... Give, and it will be given to you.... for the measure you give will be the measure you get back."

—Luke 6:37-38

Lord, she is so dirty. Her clothes are ragged, and her shoes are so big that they flip-flop when she walks. I wonder if anyone has ever given her a hug or encouragement of any kind. I know her classmates haven't. Let her be my special project this year—each and every day. Let me always keep in mind that I may be the only one to put any sunshine in her life right now. Help me to see past her appearance and smell; it's not her fault. Even as Jesus cared for lepers, let me show love to this young person. Amen.

FOR CHILDREN TO BE MORE LOVING AND ACCEPTING

Those who do not love a brother or sister whom they have seen, cannot love God whom they have not seen.

—1 John 4:20b

Jesus, even you gathered twelve close friends around you. This student has no one to talk with, eat with, or play with. I feel his loneliness. I have talked with the other children, but they have not accepted my gentle prompting. I'm not sure what to do. Show me the way to help my students open their hearts to all their classmates. Enable me to heal their spirits and make them more accepting. Amen.

WHEN A STUDENT HAS DIED

"Peace I leave with you; my peace I give to you. I do not give to you as the world gives. Do not let your hearts be troubled, and do not let them be afraid."

—*John 14:27*

One of our students is gone, Lord. Why did she have to die at such a young age? It seems so senseless to me and the friends and family who are left to cope with this tragedy. We are struggling to accept this, Lord. Comfort us and give us your peace. Amen.

FOR LATCHKEY CHILDREN

"Is there anyone among you who, if your child asks for bread, will give a stone? Or if the child asks for a fish, will give a snake?"
—Matthew 7:9-10

Lord, I know so many of my students are given their own house key and must let themselves in when they get home from school. Keep them safe from harm during the hours that they are home alone, unsupervised. Watch over them. Give them the maturity they need—but so often do not have—to make themselves a snack and start their homework. Be there for them when there is no one to hear about their day and its excitements. Let them know they are loved until their parents come home in a few hours. Amen.

FOR CHILDREN
WITHOUT A HAPPY HOME

For this is the message you have heard from the beginning, that we should love one another.
—1 John 3:11

God, only you really know what goes on in the homes of these kids. For some, I suspect abuse and mistreatment because of their behavior. I know there are drugs, alcohol, and neglect in the homes of many of them. Please give me what it takes to show love to those who never feel its warmth. These are the ones who need it most. Let school be the happy home they do not have. Amen.

FOR A STUDENT
WHOSE FATHER IS ABUSIVE

Protect me, O God, for in you I take refuge. / I say to the Lord, "You are my Lord; / I have no good apart from you."

—*Psalm 16:1-2*

Lord, he told me his dad dragged his mother out of the house by her neck, screaming, while he watched. The father hit her, kicked her, and yelled and screamed until the child told him he would kill him if he hurt his mother anymore. The father threatened to kill the child if he told. *He told,* Lord. Protect him. Amen.

FOR STUDENTS WHO ARE ILL

The LORD sustains them on their sickbed; / in their illness you heal all their infirmities.
—Psalm 41:3

It is so hard on students to miss a day of school, Lord. Give peace of mind to those who are not here today. Let them know that they can catch up on what we do while they are absent. Remind them that their friends have wondered about them and missed them today. Allow them to heal quickly and return to school as soon as possible. Amen.

WHEN I'M
NOT FEELING WELL

Have mercy upon me, O LORD; for I am weak:
O LORD, heal me.

—Psalm 6:2 KJV

Lord, I really don't belong at school today; I don't feel well. I should have stayed home to rest, but it's so much trouble to call for a substitute and write all the detailed instructions about where to find things and what to do and how to do it. Sometimes it's easier to come to work even though I cannot do the job I want to do and am capable of doing. Help me get through the day as best I can. Let my students understand that I too get sick and need their patience—just as I show them patience every day. Amen.

WHEN A TEACHER MUST BE AWAY FROM SCHOOL

The God of peace be with all of you.
—Romans 15:33

Lord, teachers are people too. Sometimes we have to be gone from our classroom. Give peace to the children in our absence. Give peace to us when we are away—whether we are dealing with illness, death, family emergencies, or personal business. Upon our return, let us pick up the pieces and go on. Amen.

FOR A SUBSTITUTE TEACHER

All of you must clothe yourselves with humility in your dealings with one another, for "God opposes the proud, / but gives grace to the humble." —1 Peter 5:5

Lord, I have to be absent from school today. It is such a temptation for the children to misbehave when I am not there. Please help them to stay on task with the lessons I have left for them to complete. Give the substitute teacher the understanding necessary to follow through with the work I have laid out.

God, being absent teaches me the lesson of humility. I like to think that I am indispensable. When I am absent, I realize that this is not true. I am reminded of my humanness. Learning will continue whether I am present or not. Thank you for the reminder. Amen.

WHEN MY EFFORTS SEEM WASTED

I can do all things through him who strengthens me.

—*Philippians 4:13*

Lord, I spent so much time on this lesson—thinking it through, planning it out, preparing the materials. What did I do wrong? As I sit and grade the follow-up practice, it seems that nearly everyone failed! I try so hard, but sometimes I feel so defeated. Help me to pick up, rethink, and regroup. Perhaps my first efforts were not the best approach. Please give me a new idea, and give me the strength and confidence to try again. Amen.

FOR ENCOURAGEMENT

Those who wait for the LORD shall renew their strength, / they shall mount up with wings like eagles, / they shall run and not be weary, / they shall walk and not faint.

—Isaiah 40:31

God, it's so long until Friday, and even longer until a holiday. Let me not give up before then. There are so many depending on me to teach them what they need to know. Even though some of them do not care and some of their parents do not cooperate, help me to remember that these are the ones who need me most. Give me the stamina I need to continue on, even though indifference is so prevalent and appreciation so rare. Help me to remember that Jesus made a miracle from the loaves and fishes and that, with little, I must teach so much and so many. Amen.

FOR SILENCE AND PEACE

"Be still, and know that I am God!"
—Psalm 46:10

It is so quiet while the students are out of the room. Let me enjoy this respite in the day. I wonder if Gethsemane was like this. Teach me to find this silence in my heart, Lord, when the children are with me, so that I may stay refreshed and continue working with them in the way that you intend. Amen.

FOR FEWER INTERRUPTIONS

May you be prepared to endure everything with patience.

—*Colossians 1:11*b

Father, how am I expected to teach when I am constantly interrupted by announcements on the intercom, students at the door, bells for recess, and papers to "immediately" sign and send somewhere? The learning process must flow like a river. Please let the river flow, Lord, without so many stops and starts, and give me more patience for the inevitable interruptions. Amen.

BEING MINDFUL OF MY POWER AND INFLUENCE

"Whoever becomes humble like this child is the greatest in the kingdom of heaven....

"If any of you put a stumbling block before one of these little ones who believe in me, it would be better for you if a great millstone were fastened around your neck and you were drowned in the depth of the sea."

—Matthew 18:4, 6

Lord, when I think about the amount of power and influence I have with my students, it frightens me. I wonder if Jesus ever felt the same way. As I teach and guide, give me humility and keep me from hurting anyone with a thoughtless word or gesture. If that should ever happen, Lord, help me to apologize and rebuild the relationship with the student I have so carelessly hurt. Amen.

IT'S OKAY TO LAUGH

A cheerful heart is a good medicine, / but a downcast spirit dries up the bones.
—*Proverbs 17:22*

They taught us in college that without discipline there is no learning. Please give me insight into this, Lord, for sometimes I cannot help laughing at the reasons my students give for misbehaving. Teach me that it is acceptable to laugh with the children and still maintain the aura of authority. Surely Jesus smiled when he talked about a camel going through the eye of a needle. Amen.

FOR MY OWN CHILDREN

Her children rise up and call her happy.
—Proverbs 31:28a

God, sometimes it is so hard for my children to have a teacher as a mother. I worry that I push them too hard, knowing how much they have to learn and how important it is for them to do well. Help me love my children for who they are, not for who I want them to be; help me show them the love, understanding, patience, and kindness that I show to my students.

As I come home each day, help me to make the transition from "teacher" to "mother," so that I do not allow my school responsibilities to push aside the responsibilities and blessings of being a mother. Amen.

BEFORE A PARENT-TEACHER CONFERENCE

Above all, clothe yourselves with love, which binds everything together in perfect harmony.
—Colossians 3:14

Lord, today I understand what Jesus meant when he said, "Let this cup pass from me; yet not what I want but what you want" (Matthew 26:39). I wish I did not have to do this. Give me the words I need to help these parents understand their child's learning problems. May I help them praise their child, even though she is not doing well in class. May I gently communicate to these parents that they too must do their part by encouraging and assisting their child at home. Assure them that I want to be their ally in their child's education, not their enemy. Allow this conference to have positive effects in the life of this child. Amen.

WHEN PARENTS ASK, "WHO IS THE BEST TEACHER IN THE NEXT GRADE?"

Why do you pass judgment on your brother or sister? Or you, why do you despise your brother or sister? For we will all stand before the judgment seat of God.... So then, each of us will be accountable to God.

—Romans 14:10, 12

Lord, how do I answer parents who ask, "Who is the best teacher in the next grade?" I know they want the best for their children, but how can I make that judgment? If I am wrong, their children's well-being is at stake. If I am unprofessional in my remarks, a coworker's reputation is at stake. Please fill me with the words I need to answer this question. I cannot find them within myself. Amen.

FOR PARENTS
WHO GET INVOLVED

*In our prayers for you we always thank God, the
Father of our Lord Jesus Christ.*

—Colossians 1:3

Almighty God, teaching is so much
easier when parents cooperate and help. It
is so hard for students to fight the
distractions of the world and get
homework done, notes signed, money
turned in, grades improved, and attitudes
adjusted! Without the help of parents,
teaching would be so much more
difficult. Thank you for these caring
parents who watch over their children and
who help me to make educating their
children a much more pleasant task.
Amen.

FOR THE PARENT-TEACHER ORGANIZATION

Let us not grow weary in doing what is right, for we will reap at harvest-time, if we do not give up. So then, whenever we have an opportunity, let us work for the good of all, and especially for those of the family of faith.
—*Galatians 6:9-10*

Lord, you know how much we appreciate the tireless efforts of those who work for the benefit of our school. Parents give of themselves so graciously to raise funds, help in the classroom, solicit donations, and contribute overall to a positive learning atmosphere. And dedicated teachers give so much of their time and energy for the welfare of their students. Without parents and teachers working together in the PTO, we would not have the quality of school we have. Amen.

FOR OUR PRINCIPAL

Where there is no guidance, a nation falls, / but in an abundance of counselors there is safety.

—Proverbs 11:14

Lord, it must be hard to always be in the middle—the middle of the children and the teachers, of the teachers and the parents, of the parents and the school board, of the school and the community. Help our principal not to lose sight of the goals for the school and the students who attend here. Give our principal the courage to stand up for what is right rather than what is easy. May the best interests of the students always be top priority as our principal guides us day by day to do the best we can do for the children. Amen.

ON GETTING
A NEW PRINCIPAL

Let each of you look not to your own interests,
but to the interests of others.
—Philippians 2:4

Heavenly Father, our school is getting new leadership. Things will change—for the better, I pray. Give me the faith I need to resist making judgments. Help me to be a good follower, giving the new principal room to make mistakes and make our school better in the process. Even Jesus stumbled under the cross. Let me not be like Thomas, who doubted, but like Peter, the Rock, and stand firmly in my classroom as a supporter of our new leader. Amen.

FOR A CLASSROOM
NEEDING REPAIRS

"Truly I tell you, just as you did it to one of the least of these . . . you did it to me."
—*Matthew 25:40*

Lord, environment is so important. I have done all I can to make this old room conducive to learning, but it is still dirty and in need of paint. I cannot afford the paint, and even if I could, when would I have time to do the work? Why is there never enough money to make all the needed repairs around here? Sometimes it seems like the students—those for whom the school exists—are the least important. Help me not to be discouraged but to remember that even if I do something for "the least of these," I have done it for you. Amen.

FRIENDSHIP
WITH A COWORKER

Beloved, let us love one another, because love is from God. —1 John 4:7a

Lord, I love my students, but living in a world of children is not easy. Sometimes I think I will never have the opportunity to read past a fourth-grade level or know more news than that found in the *Weekly Reader*. I am so grateful for the adult conversation I have with my fellow teacher, for amid this world of math facts and cursive writing, state capitals and magnets made out of nails, I have a kindred spirit—someone who knows all about kids who hear but don't listen, and someone who can laugh with me after a frustrating week of trying to explain that three plus three is not the same thing as three times three. Thank you, Lord, for my friend who reminds me that the adult world is not a bad place to be! Amen.

WHEN I'M HURT
BY A COLLEAGUE'S
HARSH WORDS

When words are many, transgression is not lacking, / but the prudent are restrained in speech. / The tongue of the righteous is choice silver. —Proverbs 10:19-20a

Lord, sometimes those we work with are so insensitive and unthinking. They say things without realizing how others will interpret them. Help me to pass off such insensitivity and move on—to learn from the experience and the hurt I feel, remembering that my own words can likewise hurt a child if I am not careful what I say.

Help me to be there for my colleagues when they are hurting. May I be a Band-Aid for my fellow teachers, just as we all are Band-Aids for the children who depend on us. Amen.

DIFFICULTIES
WITH A COWORKER

"If you love those who love you, what credit is that to you? For even sinners love those who love them. If you do good to those who do good to you, what credit it that to you? For even sinners do the same.... But love your enemies ... expecting nothing in return. Your reward will be great."
—Luke 6:32-33, 35

Lord, sometimes it is so hard to deal with my coworker. No matter how friendly I am, what I offer to share, or how hard I try to help, I am rejected. I suspect she feels threatened by my experience, but I also feel threatened by her enthusiasm. Give me the courage to keep trying to help her understand that working together benefits not only the two of us but also our students. May I look carefully at myself to see what I can do to improve our relationship. Amen.

FOR A COWORKER
ON SICK LEAVE

Thou wilt keep him in perfect peace, whose mind is stayed on thee.

—Isaiah 26:3 KJV

Lord, today we learned that our colleague will be out for several weeks due to emergency surgery. Rest within his soul and body. Give him peace and wellness of heart, so that he may accept his absence; and reassure him that learning will go on while he is away. Help him to let go, giving control to you and to the substitute teacher, so that the healing process needed to make him well may be his sole concern. Amen.

FOR PATIENCE
AND UNDERSTANDING
WHEN WORKING WITH
A DIFFICULT COLLEAGUE

My brothers and sisters, whenever you face trials of any kind, consider it nothing but joy, because you know that the testing of your faith produces endurance; and let endurance have its full effect, so that you may be mature and complete, lacking in nothing.

—*James 1:2-4*

Dear God, this colleague and I do not always see things eye to eye. Now we must work together. Please give me the patience and understanding to overcome our differences so that we may work together for the good of the students. Amen.

BEFORE AN OUT-OF-TOWN FIELD TRIP

He led them in safety, so that they were not afraid.

—*Psalm 78:53a*

Be with this group of students, parents, and teachers as we travel, O Lord. Guide us in all that we do, and allow us to return safely home. Amen.

HELP ME TO BE
A GOOD EXAMPLE

Show yourself in all respects a model of good works, and in your teaching show integrity, gravity, and sound speech that cannot be censured.

—*Titus 2:7-8*a

Thank you, O Lord, for the opportunities that you place before me each day. And thank you for the students I teach. Guide me in all that I do, so that I may set an example by doing what is right and good. Amen.

TALKING
WITH A DIFFICULT PARENT

*"Be strong and courageous; do not be frightened or dismayed, for the L*ORD *your God is with you wherever you go."*

—*Joshua 1:9*

Dear God, give me strength and confidence as I talk with a difficult parent today. Fill my heart with your Spirit, and place on my lips words that will promote a positive conversation. Amen.

FOR A SHY STUDENT

For as in one body we have many members, and not all the members have the same function, so we, who are many, are one body in Christ, and individually we are members one of another. We have gifts that differ according to the grace given to us. —Romans 12:4-6a

Dear Lord, on the most chaotic of days, she is the one child I can count on to be sitting quietly at her desk. She never speaks up, rarely asks questions, and blushes so easily. Lord, I praise her frequently—an easy thing to do—but is this enough? Guide me to gently teach her to have confidence in herself. Help me to encourage her and challenge her so that she can become the person you want her to be. You've blessed me by placing her in my class. Now help me not only to see her for what she is, but also to give her what she needs. Amen.